DIRT BIKES

Connor Dayton
Traducción al español:
Eduardo Alamán

PowerKiDS & **Editorial Buenas Letras**™
press.

New York

Published in 2007 by The Rosen Publishing Group, Inc.
29 East 21st Street, New York, NY 10010

First Edition

Editor: Jennifer Way
Book Design: Erica Clendening
Book Layout: Kate Laczynski and Lissette González
Photo Researcher: Sam Cha

Photo Credits: Cover, pp. 9, 11, 17 © John Thys/AFP/Getty Images; p. 5 © Michel Krakowski/AFP/Getty Images; p. 7, 13 © Francisco Vega/AFP/Getty Images; p. 15, 23 © www.cudbyphoto.com; p. 19 © Dan Regan/Getty Images; p. 21 © Vincent Van Doornick/AFP/Getty Images.

Cataloging Data

Dayton, Connor.
  Dirt Bikes / by Connor Dayton; traducción al español: Eduardo Alamán. — 1st ed.
     p. cm. — (Motorcycles, made for speed-Motocicletas a toda velocidad)
  Includes index.
  ISBN-13: 978-1-4042-7610-9 (library binding)
  ISBN-10: 1-4042-7610-6 (library binding)
  1. Trail bikes—Juvenile literature. 2. Motorcycles, Racing—Juvenile literature.
  3. Spanish language materials. I. Title.

Manufactured in the United States of America

CONTENTS

CONTENIDO

Dirt bikes are a type of motorcycle. They are used to race on dirt tracks.

Las *dirt bikes* son un tipo de motocicleta. *Dirt,* en español, significa tierra. Las *dirt bikes* se usan en caminos de tierra batida.

Dirt bikes have wide wheels with **grooves**. The grooves help keep the bike from **sliding** on the track's sharp turns.

Las *dirt bikes* tienen ruedas anchas con **surcos**. Los surcos hacen que la moto no se **patine** en las curvas.

Motocross is one kind of dirt bike race. Motocross races are run all over the world.

Un tipo de carrera de *dirt bike* es la de **motocrós**. Las carreras de motocrós se corren en todo el planeta.

Motocross races can get messy. Sometimes there is a lot of mud for the bike to ride through.

Las carreras de motocrós pueden ser muy sucias. A veces, la moto tiene que correr sobre mucho lodo.

Some motocross races are on dirt roads instead of on tracks.

Algunas carreras de motocrós se corren en caminos de tierra batida y no en una pista.

13

Some race tracks have big hills. This makes the race fun but more **dangerous** for the biker.

Algunas pistas tienen colinas muy altas. Esto hace que la carrera sea muy divertida, pero más **peligrosa** para el piloto.

People also do tricks on dirt bikes. They might use the bike to jump high in the air.

Los pilotos también hacen trucos con las *dirt bikes*. A veces, saltan muy alto con la motocicleta.

There are motocross games in which riders show off by doing tricks. This is called freestyle.

Hay competiciones de motocrós en las que los pilotos hacen muchos trucos. A esto se le llama estilo libre.

19

In a dirt bike race, the first biker to cross the finish line wins.

En una carrera de *dirt bikes,* el primer piloto en cruzar la línea de meta es el ganador.

The winner of a race might get a **prize**. Lots of people will take pictures of the winner.

El ganador de una carrera puede recibir un **premio**. Mucha gente toma fotografías del ganador.